Beauty Like A Rope

Advance Praise for Beauty Like A Rope

"My body has been hostage to an idea," cries Leslie St.
John, and even though this charismatic woman never loses
touch with the physical fact of the body in the world, she
is at her essence a metaphysical poet. "I'd like to rename
every body part," she insists in the first poem here, in
the hope that doing so may bring her "one day nearer
to what is unnamable." It's a brave imagination that can
face the body it lives in as both vehicle and obstacle, and
a strong mind that can transcend that dualism. But having
lost one eye in an absurd accident ("She Washed My
Hair" tells the harrowing story), Leslie St. John has let
the poet in her see with a unique third eye, one that sees
with an accurate, compassionate, wisdom-inviting gaze.
Her language is contemporary, precise and warm with
breathing; her poems offer a music that sounds intimate
even when one read aloud alone. Of special note is the
heartbreaking "Elegy for John Mark, 2002-2004," a
sequence on the death of a nephew that turns at the end
toward an unearthly lyrical beauty. But in Leslie St. John's
world, beauty is like a rope: it can rescue or kill.

~ Jim Cushing

Leslie St. John's poem, "Things that Bend," arrested me, made me eager to keep reading (Is that not part of the writer's obligation to the reader?) the poem from its first line, in which there is a lot of strong but subtle music: inch/window/sill are assonantal half-rhymes, curl/worm half rhyme, and worm/window add a little consonantal rhyme. By the fourth line, after establishing a place, she takes us to another place, the past, I believe, and an other enters the poem. It's a love poem, a poem about time and its damage, I loved the lines,

What bends short, bends long—
Doesn't break. Neck of tulip, waning
Clothes rod. And, yes, the rules.

That the heart "splinters into tributaries" is an original way of saying something all of us come to learn if we live a conscious life.

~ *Thomas Lux*

Beauty Like A Rope

Poems by
Leslie Ann St. John

First edition, May 2012
Copyright © 2012 Word Palace Press
wordpalacepress.com
wordpalacepress@aol.com

Word Palace Press
P.O. Box 583
San Luis Obispo, CA 93406

BOOK AND COVER DESIGN BY
    Ben Lawless, Penciled In Design
    penciledin.com

ISBN: 0985026049
ISBN-13:   978-0-9850260-4-2

Contents

I

3   Filling the Egg Carton
4   A Dream of Doors
6   Winter Jars
12   Reading Monet's Garden
14   Things that Bend

II

17   Elegy for John Mark, 2002-2004

III

25   The Bicyclist
27   She Washed My Hair
30   Eye Cleaning
32   Returning to the Arts Center
34   On Wanting to Speak of More than the Seasons
36   The Weight of Stories
37   Spring Fest Woodcarving

40   About Leslie St. John

ACKNOWLEDGEMENTS

Thanks to the editors of the following journals:

APERCUS QUARTERLY
A Dream of Doors
CIMARRON REVIEW
Eye Cleaning, Returning to the Arts Center
INDIANA REVIEW
Reading Monet's Garden, Spring Fest Woodcarving
INKWELL
Filling the Egg Carton
ROUGAROU
Apology
THE MACGUFFIN
Things that Bend, The Bicyclist, Loving You Departed...
THE PINCH
On Wanting to Speak of More...

Beauty Like A Rope

I

Filling the Egg Carton

My real name is Lucinda.
Yesterday my name was *speaks with no sound*.
Tomorrow my name will be *centrifuge*,
head pinned in a mental halo. My mother
thinks my name is *prodigal daughter*;
my nephew, *crazy california*. In dreams
my name is *whispers in gloaming*.
And though he knows my name
is *Lago Bianco*, my lover never says it.
He wades deep in my waters,
cautious of the undertow.

      I'd like to rename
every body part: fingers, *apple-pickers*;
back, *Waipi'o Valley*; heart, *opal weed*;
Stomach, I made you Lucinda's urn,
filled you with shaved shale and apology
cards sent to no one. If today, I name you
that which remains and invite a child close
to wipe her cheeks across my soft center,
will I be the arbitrator of loneliness,
one day nearer what is unnamable?

A Dream of Doors

I'd like to take a tour of doors: scrolling wrought iron
in Paris, heavy brass in Italy, carved oak in the Carolinas.

I'd like to touch doorknobs: green medallions,
brass faded like good jeans. Coolness and click
of a lock sliding open, fingers wrap handle,

thumb depresses a metal tongue and presto! Open.
I'd like to feel myself on one side of things and then

the other. I'd like to hear the pentatonic scale
played back to me as I knock on a hundred doors.
I'd like to hear the wind pull a door shut,

ease a door open. I could unscrew hinges
and remove a door completely, feel the open mouth

of a house gape at my indiscretion. I'd like to stand
in the frame, waving goodbye as he rides his bike away,
a tiny bell wave back. I would do gravestone etchings

of dates, manufacturers, names engraved, birds flying
from nowhere to somewhere, and I'd paper my door

with the impressions of doors from Tippicanoe county
or string them across my porch like prayer flags.
I'd like to see my dog nosing the door open

to jump her face closer once more. Give me
a garland of red doors strung across a blue sky,

let birds fly through and paper planes; may a kite catch
and hang in the frame. Let the door swing wide and pour
a tumbler of milk onto a willow tree, its arms of hair

heavy with nourishment, my hand outstretched
to catch whatever may fall.

Winter Jars

I.

He tried to carry my dog, her body
wrapped in a sheet, blood from her crushed
teeth, lungs, heart, what
white cotton, purple tears...

Someone else planted an orange tree.
Someone else gifted a white orchid,
the heavy stems I've already broken—

soil and bark spilled over hardwood,
white petals like a felled petticoat—

and braced with twisty ties and binder
clips, whatever to hold it in place:
column of window light, clay disc
of her paw impression, wooden urn,

at the foot of my bed, the morning offering,
at the foot of my bed, evening prayers,
afternoon regrets, 3:00am regrets—

the rituals hold me in place,
or they hold a place I can't yet fill.

Am I talking about my eleven-year
her, my cold-nose-warm breath her?

My head is an outdoor tub,
brimmed with wet leaves in perpetual fall.

2.

It's just a little wind disturbing
a small circle of water, this
culmination of touch.

Imagine for months, then one
unchecked night, touch becomes
tentative teeth on cold tile.

My hip. I placed his hand there first.
My stomach. And he lingered,
measured me like a tool, turning

me this way, checking to see if the weight
is right in his hand, if the fit is good.
He stayed, his only assertion.

He stayed after two movies, closing
credits, looping introduction,
and I ran my hand along his torso—

a tight, thin, elegant torso,
more like a piece of art than
the body of a man. My body

has been hostage to an idea
and now released, the idea's hold
persists, where his new hand makes a circle,

where your head used to be.
But I'll own it. I wanted him near
and closer, the 3:00am nap, my removed bra.

I went up the hill to a white house,
his hand climbing inside me, my chest lifting higher.

3.

From over Dallas, Christmas lights
script tattoos on an ancient god,
the black ground his flesh; his face
too far behind or somewhere far ahead.

Record onto a tape and play it back:
My heart is an abandoned zoo.
My heart is…

Gates opening and closing with wind,
only shadows pace behind bars,
tank water thins to more wet leaves,
yellowed feathers, their brief stencils.

"And that other heart?" I ask.
"You mean the soul in fool's gold?"
"Yes, that one." "It's a ghost town,
everyone gone, or just too far away."

4.

I wonder if you're in a cold lab,
still leaning over flattened, stripped plants,
numbering their life codes into a manageable order,
"grasping," as you say, for "progress and discovery,"
while I am fixed to the wooden pew, sun blasting

shadeless windows, then not, whole days rolling on
in meaningless decisions: I'll take peppermint tea,
I'll mail the box, I'll mark many tests...
until I'm dropped into a beaker of solution,
one red tail spreading like a song, think of me.

5.

What to do with winter jars
in Spring? Sit them in the windowsill,
watch jasmine wither to dust?

Pennies dull in sunlight? I've tracked you
in a red-tailed hawk, empty blue sky
to power line, perched and readied.

I've heard the laughter of playground
antics and felt Clair's swift ghost circle
my feet in grass-tearing bouts of joy.

I've even read a story under gathering
fog-clouds, two goosefleshed bodies
poised for what? The sacrament?

God, not a monologue but flesh,
scrambled eggs and wine. I've not the mind
to say anything of my generation,

Only what's pocketable for one,
maybe two. I touch silver streamers
waving from high windows,

Believing myself able to fly.
trade one fallacy for another,
the street scene still disintegrates.

Jars remain full and sealed
or I empty them of dialogue,
one gray hair left on a pillow,

Counterfeit metro tickets,
scrub-jay feathers, songs sung
under breath, the last hour milking

into blue.

Reading Monet's Garden

It's not the feathery willows or artichoke
roses or even the purple-green water-lilies
shaped like blood cells under a microscope

that interest me—it's the boat he made:
a place to see, to paint, to get away from
eight children and not one but two wives

(even if it wasn't legal until Camille died
from child-birth complications, *having been*
tenderly cared for by Alice—the other wife.)

Perhaps it's morning before the kids wake
or afternoon when Camille and Alice argue
over what to order: more poultry or fish.

Monet has already walked the garden twice.
Unsteady in his boat, he steps lightly toward
the bow, removes a satchel of peaches,

considers the blackness of leather boots
on brown wood and, in turn, deficiencies
in his handling of darker colors. In plein air

the golden eyes of irises follow him
as he passes slowly. The imperceptible
sway of water-wake blurs the points

of grasses and ferns. The granite-walled pond
makes duplicates of bamboo and weeping-
willows. To be surrounded by a mirror-garden,

to move through it, is to feel the vibration
of every bird landing on a limb or parting
pliant leaves. A frog makes widening

tree rings on the surface of the water. All
afternoon and the board he's sitting on
becomes harder, but his seeing softens.

Beyond the geometry of a Japanese bridge,
two bodies reach for each other, touch,
and fade into loose patches of dark turquoise.

I see something of what he saw: the impossibility
of division, of separating red shawl and woman,
of choosing one garden view over another.

Things that Bend

~ *After Dorianne Laux's "What's Broken"*

The inch worm in the window sill, curling
In a bank of light. Snow-soaked porch steps,

Old pinewood floors. The neck, the back—
My body bends into another body. Firelight

Bends around his shoulders, a half-moon
Around stars, around the tops of trees.

We are both the driver on dark highways
Breaking for bends in the road, and the river

Rushing over rocks toward the bend ahead.
What bends short, bends long—

Doesn't break. Neck of tulip, waning
Clothes rod. And, yes, the rules.

Because the heart is not straight and narrow.
It curves, sometimes splinters into tributaries,

Carrying all the waste of a community of two:
Words like dead fish floating to the surface,

Gills closed, eyes fixed. But the mouth opens
Like a fresh bruise—purple, bell-shaped—

And you forget yourself, your heart
A wire hanger bending in someone's hands.

II

Elegy for John Mark, 2002-2004

I.

John Mark's Frogs

The birthday plates were green to match the cake. The
gifts, wrapped in paper of a thousand frogs, were tucked
away in the hall closet. My niece says he carried frogs
everywhere—even in the bath. I remember his deathday
but not his birthday. I am an aunt four states away who
didn't hear his bare feet slap the hardwood floors the way
my sister does now when she feels his ghost. *During the
bedtime story and snack, he choked on a pretzel and stopped
breathing. In the helicopter from Forth Smith to Little Rock, his
brain began to swell, cells began to starve, and in days, his arm
and leg were black.* His hospital bed faced the entry, so there
was no way to brace myself for the smallest patient, the
tubes and bandages, the garden of frogs blooming from
every window sill, shelf, and chair. His breath was barely
perceptible, only the black accordion beside him moving
in respiration-rhythm. As we age our bodies lose moisture:
our joints tighten, our skin sags and shrivels. He was only
two. There should be a blue pond in his belly. After thirty-
two days, the family gathered to hear his death-breath. No
one expected him to live for eight more days, spooned
by his mother in a bed with no tubes and no lights. The
machines silent. His elderly smoker's breath rattling her
own chest.

II.

I speak into the phone and hear myself on the Apology Hotline:

"I'm sorry for…
    putting the empty pitcher back in the fridge
    being too tired tonight, this headache
    saying she sang "well"
    throwing your class ring across the street
    laughing at the funeral
    not picking up the dog poop
    locking you out
    giving your bible away
    buying designer jeans
    forgetting your birthday and yours and yours
    not hoisting my nephew on my hip
    clichéd phone conversations
    drinking Starbucks coffee
    thinking of fish as swimming vegetables
    the paper I will use to print this poem
    the time I didn't spend calling my father, mother, sisters
    not rinsing the peanut butter spoon
    the sag in the bookshelf and my clothes rod
    never touching someone with AIDS
    never even knowing someone with it
    global warming, drought,
    not responding to your email
    not being clever or able to hold my martinis

missing your show
staring at your prosthesis
the cancer in your breast
worrying more if it will metastasize to mine
moving away before I heard my nephew say, "Asparagus"
the shrapnel scars on my cousin's leg
not reading *Moby-Dick* or *Huckleberry Finn*
mocking your small-town religion
arriving ten minutes late
hiding your credit card in my sock drawer
using my credit card
the deficit and not knowing what it is
not taking the day trip to Florence
fighting over a map in downtown Roma
Superman's death, how we almost missed it
How your two-year-old son's death didn't come
    after you turned off the machines, but eight days
        later, his breathing like a wave's close-out,
            tumbling rocks, sand, arms and legs."

III.

J.M.W.
>   *The sound of the needle*
> *hushing over clear vinyl after the record ends.*
>   *~ Jane Hirshfield*

Whenever I see a bag of pretzels,
I see a shard small as a fingernail
clipping, lodged in his trachea,
how the fluid filled his lungs.

My nephew in PICU, thirty-two days:
the smell of latex on his purpling arms,
his pink tongue, spotted black,
to the side of a feeding tube,
his swollen eyes with half moons
of lubricant from corner to corner.

And what if his nearly translucent hair,
dusk eyes, and thick cheeks stopped
morphing into every child
I meet in the grocery store, laundry mat?

What things will we forget?
Transparent pebbles of water
about to boil, the weight of a wet
shirt when first lifted from the sink.

Your whole leg was shorter than my arm.

IV.

Apology

> *For burial the Chinese fill*
> *the seven openings of the body with white jade.*

Forgive my opening—the eye, the mouth,

the other mouth. You couldn't have known

that I removed the white jade and placed

the stones in your pockets.

But didn't you notice the weight,

smoothness under your thumb, clap

of rock and bone? I didn't just dream

of you singing while tightrope walking

the shadow of a power line—

I wanted to cut your hair in the kitchen,

feel downy curls fall on my bare feet.

V.

Loving You Departed Does Not Mean Death

Because I Still See

Yellow leaves like whispers stretching from a shallow swamp
An old Chinese woman practicing tai chi on the playground

Because I Still See

Grasses fanning and folding like my nephew's hair underwater
Ice flows in a dirty river parting and coming together, hissing

Because I Still See

Indian widows dancing, painting each others' faces canary yellow
Leaves thin as onion skins, shiny as frosted ornaments in sunlight

Because I Still See

Men meeting men in Dolores park with their lean dogs fetching
Words in the snow — *beauty, truth* — easily as faces in the stars

Because I Still See

A rainbow of koi swimming under the red half-moon bridge
Where you took off your shoes and stepped on slippery stones

Because I Still See

Loving you in cold water reaching for a handful of watercress
Weeds and small white flowers tangled beneath the surface

III

The Bicyclist

A young girl takes the corner of Roberts
and 12th while standing straight-legged
on pedals. Her hands lightly around
handle bars—an easy confidence—her head
turned away from the turn she's making,
wind lifting sun-and-chlorine-streaked hair.
She's not alone: a boy rides a scooter,
other kids on bikes, but she possesses
something they don't, her muscled,
hair-sheened legs, the flexed arches
of her feet, how she leans into wind
like it's an elastic band ready to rebound
her fall. She will come to knowledge
differently than the others.

It will cost her more. Men will bite
into the geometry of her shoulders
and collarbones, press into the sway
of her back, tell her *not now* and *ready*
and *come*. And women, they will take
from her—Mothers will advise
their daughters to *run with other girls*,
breakroom coworkers will stare
at an unfastened button on her blouse
through the rising steam of microwave
meals and eventually suggest she
"Do something about *that*."

And I want to lean over the rusted
chain-link fence, tell her to stop,
say, *Your kind of beauty is too much
for us*. Instead, she opens her mouth
quick as a kickstand and asks, "Do you
know where Megan Silverman lives,
the house with the blue shutters?"
I tell her to keep going for two more
blocks, then turn right and right again.
I tell her because it's all I can say.

She Washed My Hair

After the corn snake lines to Cornerstone,
a Christian music festival in Bushnell, IL;

after the ska show under the big tent;
after skankin' and cheers and beach balls
bouncing over our heads, the CD case

struck my eye, expelling green iris and lens
to the dirt; after the body-pushing, rope-

tripping, car-maze walk to the first aid trailer;
after the cold vinyl, potholed van ride
to the hospital; after the 2:00am operation

on the Fourth of July, the forty-two stitches;
after my newly divorced father and mother

drove across four states—a pillow barrier
between them to bring me home
to Arkansas, the new room my aunts

assembled from what was still in boxes
in the garage: Monet's lily pads on the wall,

music box on the chest of drawers, winter
clothes in the closet, a gold-leafed gift book
on the nightstand: *He will wipe every tear*

from your eye. He will make the blind to see again.

After the month of casseroles and cards; after
my father's only visit, two-dozen stargazer lilies;

after Dr. Medcliff injected
an expandable bubble of gas in my eye
to seal the retina, raise the pressure; after days

of lying on my left side to eat saltine crackers,
drink sprite, stare out the window and watch

summer slip away like an apology,
all the while trying not to cough
or sneeze or hiccup and burst my chance;

after walking to the restroom head bent
like a thin poplar in wind, trying hard

not to disturb the tightrope act in my eye—
that I might see, that I might
keep the eye, face intact;

after Mom raised my lid to drop medicine,
she washed my hair,

untangling rusted screw curls, not with force
as she had after dance recitals
and ice skating competitions, but with care—

a jeweler unknotting a thin gold chain,
rubbing each kink smooth.

Her small hand supported my head
dangling from the foot of the bed,
the other tipping an iced tea pitcher

of water to rinse the shampoo.
So, how to tell her now—

twelve years, two states, one husband,
and three prosthetic eyes later—
she made me feel even this loss as love?

Eye Cleaning

The ocularist comes at me,
with the narrow suction cup,
a sixth finger. This prosthetic eye,
molded, painted, fired.

Every three months, I drive an hour
to have it cleaned, to have someone else
lift the top lid with his index finger, pull
down the lower lid with his thumb
toggle it out like a game piece.

The hole in my face just big enough
for a buckeye nut, like the one
in my father's desk drawer.
He'd shown me how to *rub worries away*
running his thumb over the smooth,
wood-eye for luck. *Keep it in your pocket*,
he'd said, *our secret kryptonite*.

But I have only balled lint in my pocket,
nothing in my eye-socket. Just cool
acidic oxygen filling in all the gaps
where a gray-green iris should be,
my prom night without a patch.

Once I locked myself in the bathroom,
tried to clean it: ten minutes, thirty, an hour.

It was a button that wouldn't fasten,
my eyelid stitched too tight, the eye
too large. The coin slot of pink flesh
never meant to be reflected in a mirror.

Dr. Hetzler rinses hypoallergenic soap
from the polycarbonate eye,
like one would wash dishes, or massage
away a headache. He rubs his thumb over
the raised pupil, the concave back
like it might bring him luck.

Returning to the Arts Center

People take photos under an open-air trellis,
talk on cell phones near the *Imploding Cube*,
wear sunglasses, shorts, sneakers, crunch
gravel under their feet while speaking of
falling leaves, their daughters' dorm décor.
What's most different is that you're not here.
The rock on which I lie stomach down is not
your solid chest and narrow waist, the breeze
on my shoulder is not your breath. I believed
you when you said *The art is great, but you're*
the most beautiful thing here, because I'm in need
of evidence that this body is more than injury
and utility. I place my palms flat over the eyes
of a bronze and concrete *Black Titan*, my fingers
curve over the thick arc of bone and brow.
Yes, the right eye is smaller. You didn't believe me
then, both our hands rubbing cool deep-set
eyes the size of two varieties of tulip bulbs.
Did Spaulding sculpt injury? His? Someone
else's? Mine? I only ask as one who's fixed
her chin on the leather strap of an AP100
and forced her eyes to remain open as a doctor
removed forty-two stitches from the sclera
surface and barely-there iris with metal tweezers
the size of child chopsticks. He'd told me
to stare into the blue light, shadows of fingers
and tweezers fanned across the warm dot
like moths to a porch light. I ask as one who's

felt her right eye shrinking in its socket,
softening over time like a tongued fireball.
I want to know if this Titan saw his fingers
through a dark tunnel one day and nothing
the next. If he wiped sweat and ointment
from behind a gauzy patch, while thinking
of all his body parts, how some are dispensable –
an eye finally discarded in a red plastic bag.
I want to be pressed hard against this freshly
laid sod behind me, to feel the shifting soil
underneath as something solid, braided roots
a net that will hold my body if I kneel,
to say okay to the sadness hardened here
behind the Black Titan's mismatched eyes.

On Wanting to Speak of More than the Seasons

In the space under the deck
    where cats go to give birth
        and die, I made finger-width holes

in the dirt, planted white buttons,
    sugar cubes, tablets of aspirin.
        My father told me not to crawl under

the house where he dug up
    potatoes, stored kayaks, buried
        what? Christmas tins of rolled

hundred dollar bills? Letters
    or maybe receipts from another
        life? What will grow in shadows,

bands of hot light through cracked
    boards? The sticky web of a black
        widow? A sugar-tree with button leaves?

In my converted bedroom,
    a dining room with floor-to-ceiling
        windows colored in with nighttime,

I felt the ghosts of television aliens,
saber-toothed Easter bunnies,
even the silent, towering pines

pressing against the glass, fogging
a cloud of breath. But now in my thirtieth
year, five states away, I know

nothing is darker than a closed mouth,
words locked in the moist house of wanting.

The Weight of Stories

She wakes and holds her handlebar hips,
reviews last night's salmon bisque and wine,
forgets the weight of stories, steps lightly to the scale,

revisits men who clutch her 26 inch waist, shift
into gear, and drive her pelvis like a red corvette.
She wakes and holds her handlebar hips,

repeats the double-zero blond—cigarette
in flower petal lips—the philosopher chose instead,
forgets the weight of stories, steps lightly to the scale,

replays mother spooning ice cream at the freezer,
spandex stretched across a continent of longing.
She wakes and holds her handlebar hips,

remembers father in the mirror, side-angle view
exposing a sucked-in stomach: *let it go, let us be*—
forgets the weight of stories, steps lightly to the scale.

She almost feels rainwater collecting in her bones,
her hummingbird heart beating against windows,
but again, she wakes and holds her handlebar hips,
rewinds every story, steps lightly to the scale.

Spring Fest Woodcarving

I think about scissor-snipping corners
of grade school snowflakes while watching
this guy as he finds rhythm with a 25 lb. chainsaw,
shrill powerhead, sprockets, loops of chain
wheeling under his light, measured touch.
He moves in, pulls back, side-steps
all the way around the sectioned tree
trunk. Then does it again. Sawdust,
a small wave in his wake.

His bluing Arkansas flag tattoo shows under
his faded T-shirt. Safety glasses and leather
chaps. Large chunks fall from the sides. This
is performance art, the beauty of a thing
becoming with each shallow cut.

Not the life-size bear with *1605 Lemoncrest Ln.*
burned in its belly, not the bust of Lord Jesus
himself: his long face rawboned, grandfatherly.
It is something I've never seen, how sun
whitens the inside of pine. A slip
of the blade takes him away from the traced line.
He must follow the unseen path error makes,
slivering wood until the block becomes
almost human, smaller
and smaller now.

I am waiting for that moment when the form
announces itself. He wipes wood chips and
dust from soft-fist chin, double lines of lips,
thin nose bone. She is looking beyond
him, past other oaks and maples.

About Leslie St. John

A native of Little Rock, AR, Leslie St. John received her M.F.A. from Purdue University, where she served as poetry editor for Sycamore Review. Her poems have appeared in *Cimarron Review, Crab Orchard Review, Florida Review, Indiana Review, Linebreak, Pinch*, and *Verse Daily*. Her nonfiction has appeared in *Opium* and *Relevant*. She was nominated by Lisa Lewis and Ai for a Pushcart Prize. She won the 12th National *MacGuffin* Poet Hunt contest. Mark Doty chose her poem "Filling the Egg Carton" as a finalist for the 2010 *Inkwell* Poetry Prize. That same year, she completed her 200-hour Prajna yoga teacher training with Tias Little of Santa Fe, NM. As part of her *Svadhyaya* self-study, she wrote a memoir/research essay on the relationship between yoga and eating disorders; she continues this exploration in her poems and essays. As a yogi and modern dancer, Leslie is interested in seeing the intersections between poetry and the body—during the creative process and within developed poems. Currently, she is teaching a yoga and creative writing workshop called "Poses and Prose." She teaches English at Cal Poly in San Luis Obispo, CA.

Made in the USA
San Bernardino, CA
01 January 2016